Midnight Forest

COLORING BOOK

Animal Designs on a Dramatic Black Background

LINDSEY BOYLAN

DOVER PUBLICATIONS, INC.
MINEOLA, NEW YORK

The Midnight Forest is the habitat of the most amazing creatures! You'll find a baying wolf, a gentle deer, a pair of butterflies, wide-eyed owls, and many more forest dwellers—each one sporting a splendid decoration of floral and abstract designs. Adding to the excitement is the intense black background on every page, as well as the exotic forest foliage. Just select your media and experiment with the colors of your choice as you enjoy the creative possibilities of this unique collection—plus, the perforated, unbacked pages make displaying your work easy!

Bibliographical Note

Midnight Forest Coloring Book: Animal Designs on a Dramatic Black Background is a new work, first published by Dover Publications, Inc., in 2015.

International Standard Book Number

ISBN-13: 978-0-486-80500-9
ISBN-10: 0-486-80500-X

Manufactured in the United States by RR Donnelley
80500X02   2015
www.doverpublications.com